SIMPLY SCOTTISH
Cakes & Bakes

Karon H Grieve

FORTH BOOKS

This book is dedicated to my mum with much love and many thanks.

First published in the UK in Hardback 2012
This Paperback edition, 2021, 2024
by Forth Books
www.forthbooks.co.uk

Text copyright Karon H Grieve 2024
Photographs copyright Karon H Grieve 2024

The authors' moral rights have been asserted.
All rights reserved. No part of this publication may be reproduced, stored in a retrieval system, or transmitted in any form or by any means, electronic, mechanical, photocopying or otherwise, without the prior permission of the publisher.

ISBN 978-1-909266-21-6

Printed in India

A CIP record of this book is available from the British Library.

Visit Karon on her daily blog at www.karongrieve.com

Some recipes may contain nuts.

Also available as an ebook - 978-1-909266-02-5

my thanks

Writing a cook book is a law unto itself, it's not just you and a computer, words and paper, there are so many people involved in testing and tasting and helping you get it right. I'd like to take this opportunity to thank them here;

Firstly to Crawford and Jackie of Forth Books for asking me to do all this in the first place. You placed a lot of faith in me and I hope it has been rewarded.

To my long suffering daughter Idgy for being so patient while I wrote this book and for putting up with me when the kitchen was covered in flour and sugar and there was nothing in the fridge but butter. You are the reason I bake, cook, write, live, smile and get up in the morning.

To all my friends (and Idgy's too) who tried out all the recipes and donned all those calories.

To my blog readers who always inspire me and encourage me to keep going even when I think I've lost the plot.

To you, the reader, for holding this book and hopefully trying out the recipes and having a go.

And most of all thanks to my mum, for showing me how to bake, I miss you.

Contents

Introduction
Baking Basics
Breads & Bannocks
Simply Scones
A Piece of Cake
A Wee Cake
What A Tart
Just Ginger
Specially Shortbread
Taking the Biscuit
Finishing Touches
Index

introduction

If Scottish baking conjures up only images of scones, oatcakes and shortbread for you, then you really need to read on and find out about all the other gorgeous goodies our fine country has to offer the baking world.

From classics like Crulla and Almond Flory to my own Cranachan Cheesecake and Porridge Pancakes, there really is something for everyone with a sweet tooth and an appetite for the good things in life.

Baking is becoming more and more popular, for many it is something of a novelty, a hobby, a pleasure to be enjoyed in their spare time. But not so long ago home baking was a necessity, a chore that many could well do without.

My Mum showed me how to bake. She didn't teach me, she showed by her own everyday example. My mum made cakes and pies, rolls and scones. No Sunday was complete without a frushie of some sort gracing the dinner table; no cup of tea was ever suggested without a scone or a 'bit o'cake' to soak it up.

Baking was just there; it was never saved just for big occasions like birthdays or Christmas, although on those days it was extra special, it was just how we had sweet things and puddings around the house. I will never forget my mum's total horror when I reported back after tea at a friend's house that they had the most amazing cake 'from a supermarket', wow, this was such a treat to me. My poor mother was scandalised that anyone should even think of buying any sort of cake, and from a supermarket, whatever next!

Times change and nowadays you can buy almost anything in a supermarket, including very nice cakes and pastries from all over the world. However, there is something really special about home baking; to me it is comfortable magic. Taking a handful if assorted mismatched ingredients, bringing them together, adding a little heat and timing, and hey presto – you have produced something worthy of the finest magicians – but much better than any rabbit popping out of a hat, your magic tastes delicious and brings smiles all round.

The following pages contain over fifty of my favourite Scottish baking recipes. All are simple to work with, just read the recipe, make sure you have all your ingredients to hand before you start, and take your time – enjoy the process as much as the results. Please don't be daunted by the list of ingredients in the Black Bun or Dundee Cake, it might look like a lot on paper, but really it's just a mix of different dried fruits and spices, I just have to list them all individually so it can look a bit scary to the beginner, fear not, it's all easy.

To maintain the easy theme I have taken the liberty of using store bought puff pastry for a couple of recipes. It really is made to such a high standard nowadays and does save you that extra bit of time in the kitchen.

I have also included ten recipes for those little finishing touches like jams and jellies that make your bakes extra special.

So welcome to Simply Scottish – Cakes & Bakes, I hope you will try out the recipes, tweak them to suit your own taste buds and come away knowing that baking in Scotland contains some truly wonderful scones, oatcakes and shortbreads and a lot more besides.

Karon H Grieve
Ayrshire, Scotland 2012

Baking Basics

words and ways

If you are already a keen cook you will probably know all of these terms, but for those who are new to baking it's good to know what on earth recipes are talking about.

paper work
baking paper/parchment is for lining your tins to avoid food sticking to them. Often sold as 'non stick' which saves you a job. Makes removal of cakes etc really easy and saves on all the chiselling off if you've accidently burned something – we all do!
greaseproof paper use this in the same way as baking paper, just always remember to grease it first.

powders
baking powder is a mixture of bicarbonate of soda and cream of tartar. It works by bubbling up when liquid is added producing carbon dioxide which then expands in the heat of the oven and gives your cakes that light and airy texture.
bicarbonate of soda one part of the above mixture, this is gentler but still gives a lift.
cream of tartar super fast acting raising agent that springs into action the moment it touches liquid.

flours
cornflour is used in shortbread if you don't have rice flour. Also used as a thickening agent in sauces etc. A very fine flour.
plain flour is your standard flour for baking. It contains no raising agents at all so if you want cakes to rise you must add those yourself.
rice flour is beautifully fine and often used as part of the mix in shortbreads.
self-raising flour is plain flour that has already had raising agents added into it. Great for sponges and light mixes.
strong plain flour is your average bread making flour and gives just the right texture for breads.
wholemeal flours have a nuttier taste and contain the bran from the flour. They are good for extra flavour in fruit cakes, breads etc.

oatmeal
I have used medium oatmeal in all but one recipe (Porridge Pancakes – where I have used instant porridge oats), please note that oatmeal is not the same as porridge oats. The latter are rolled oats already part steamed for quicker cooking. They have less flavour than true oatmeal.

sugar, sugar
Not just a sweetener this actually helps to give your bakes texture too, so always use the right sugar for the job.
caster sugar can be either white (refined) or golden (unrefined), it is very fine and creams easily.
demerara sugar is golden brown in colour and very grainy.
granulated sugar is the stuff you usually use to sweeten your tea; it is very grainy and does not blend or dissolve easily. Save it for the tea or for scattering as a topping.
icing sugar is a powdered sugar that is extremely fine. Always sift it as it tends to form little clumps and lumps in the packet.
muscovado sugar is dark and soft and rich with a wonderfully strong flavour.
soft light or *dark brown sugars* have a richer flavour than caster sugar and cream really well with butter. Often used in fruit cakes.

in the mix
beating is when you soften ingredients (ie butter) and then you use a wooden spoon, whisk or mixer to mix things together and add air at the same time.
blending is when two or more ingredients are thoroughly mixed together.
creaming is when you mix butter and sugar together to make them light and fluffy before adding other ingredients. This really lightens the texture of your finished product so always do it when recipe calls for it.
folding is when you have already have your creamed mixture and want to add flour etc. Use a large metal spoon and slice into the mixture and turn it over. You can also use a figure of eight motion. This keeps the air in the mix but brings the ingredients together.
kneading is good exercise, it is when you bring the outside of the dough into the centre, fold over, press and pummel and do it again and again. This strengthens the gluten in the flour and gives more elasticity and eventually a good rise to the dough.
knocking back is a term used when you are making breads and have already kneaded the dough and left it to rise. You are just kneading again to knock out any big air pockets so that the dough will bake evenly.
proving is where you leave the bread dough a second time after knocking back and before you put it in the oven to bake.
rubbing in is what you do with butter and flours to make scones, biscuits and shortcrust pastry. Use a light touch and just your fingertips. You want to rub together the butter and flours until they look like breadcrumbs.
sifting is where you shake your dry ingredients through a metal or plastic sieve to remove any lumps and to allow for more air to be incorporated. I like to sieve my flours when baking.

whipping is where you really use speed (either elbow grease or electricity!) to stir air into a something like cream.

hot stuff

I have listed the oven temperature for each recipe. If you are using a fan assisted oven then reduce the temperature by about 10% and check with your manufacturer's manual as to whether you have to reduce the cooking time too as these ovens can vary.

preheating the oven is very important. The times given are for an oven that is already at that temperature. Always think 'oven' before you get your ingredients out – be prepared!

too hot an oven will mean that your bakes will burn outside before the inside has had a chance to cook properly.

too cool can cause things to rise unevenly and sink in the middle.

just checking – we all love to open that oven door 'just to check' how our bakes are doing. Don't do this until at least half way through the baking time as the change in temperature as you open the door will interrupt the rising process and this could cause cakes to sink and bake unevenly.

Measures

Cake dish sizes

Metric	Imperial
15cm	6in
18cm	7in
20cm	8in
23cm	9in

Loaf dish sizes

Metric	Imperial
23x12cm	9x5in
25x8cm	10x3in
28x18cm	11x7in

Liquid measures

Metric	Imperial	Cup & Spoon
mL millilitres	fl oz fluid ounce	
5mL	1/6fl oz	1 teaspoon
20mL	2/3fl oz	1 tablespoon
30mL	1fl oz	1 tablespoon plus 2 teaspoons
60mL	2fl oz	1/4 cup
85mL	2 1/2fl oz	1/3 cup
100mL	3fl oz	3/8 cup
125mL	4fl oz	1/2 cup
150mL	5fl oz	1/4 pint, 1 gill cup
250mL	8fl oz	
300mL	10fl oz	1/2 pint
360mL	12fl oz	1 1/2 cups
420mL	14fl oz	1 3/4 cups
500mL	16fl oz	2 cups
600mL	20fl oz 1 pint,	2 1/2 cups
1 litre	35fl oz 1 3/4 pints,	4 cups

Oven temperatures:
120°C	(250°F)	
140°C	(275°F)	Gas 1/2
150°C	(300°F)	Gas 1
170°C	(325°F)	Gas 2
180°C	(350°F)	Gas 4
190°C	(375°F)	Gas 5
200°C	(400°F)	Gas 6
220°C	(425°F)	Gas 7

tools and tips – tool box basics

Cooks always have their favourite tools that they use all the time, these become like old friends and wooden spoons are a prime example. They just seem to get better with age.
There is no need to have an armoury of every kitchen gadget known to man, you can keep things pretty simple for baking so there is no need to rush out and spend a fortune.
Here are the basic items you'll need and some tips on how to use them.

tins and trays
Don't just think of this as a piece of metal to hold your mix and throw into the oven. Your baking tins are of the utmost importance. Good solid heavy trays are best as they will withstand the full blast of the oven without buckling under the heat. Cheaper thin trays will often warp and can mean that your bakes will heat unevenly and cause poor results. Invest in the best tins you can.
If a tin is not of the non-stick variety then you must grease and line it before use. Even with modern non-stick bakeware I still like to grease and line my tins. It just makes removal and clean up that bit easier and I am all for that.
Preparing a tin
To measure a cake tin simply place it on top of your greaseproof paper and draw around the bottom with a pencil. Cut out the shape and this will fit perfectly into the base of your tin.
To line the sides just cut a strip of greaseproof paper 1cm higher than the tin height and wrap it around to get the length you require. Cut it 1-2cm longer than required so that you have a little overlap.
Use a pastry brush and either melted butter or vegetable oil to paint the entire surface of the tin. Place the base paper in first and then your side paper.
For straight sides tins (loaf, square, oblong etc) I like to take a piece of greaseproof paper and sit the tin on top, make sure that the paper comes up higher than the top edge of the tin on either side (the longer sides for loaf/rectangle) and cut out. This gives you coverage on base and both long sides of tin and also extra to hold on to either side and lift the bake out of the tin after cooking.
For fruit cakes I like to use a double thickness of greaseproof paper to protect the cake while it cooks.
Make sure you clean your tins after every use, even with baking paper of some sort you will get residue on the tin so wash before storing.

cooling rack
Nobody likes a soggy bottom so I really cannot stress enough the value of a wire rack for cooling your bakes. This applies while cake is both in and out of the tin, use your rack! So many cakes are ruined by turning out too soon on to a solid plate. Cakes and bakes need to have air

circulating all around to cool properly, besides, they cool quicker this way and protect your kitchen surfaces too.

scales
Use measuring scales and use only one type of measure, either metric or imperial. Don't mix up both within the same recipe as they are not exact translations.

measuring spoons
These are another Must Have item. You cannot get away with normal serving spoons as measuring devices; you really must use proper measuring spoons.

wooden spoons
I have a thing about old wooden spoons; I just love the patina as they age. That aside, you can't beat a wooden soon for beating!

metal spoons
For folding in your flour etc after you have beaten the butter and sugar together. A metal spoon cuts into the batter and gets right to the bottom of the bowl. When you are folding in flour you want to be able to really cut into the mix, lift it up and fold it over.

oven thermometer
If you have an old cooker it is well worth the small investment to buy one of these little gizmos. Very often old ovens can be out as much as 15 degrees, so it is worth being able to check your temperatures.

palette knife
This is a must for getting the last scrape of batter from bowls and for lifting reluctant baked goodies from tins.

oven gloves
Does this sound like I am preaching to the converted here? Maybe so, but the number of people who have had accidents by using a tea towel instead of proper oven gloves to remove hot trays from the oven is astounding. Oven gloves are specially made to protect and grip. A tea towel is not, be warned.

tea towels
Yes of course they have their uses, and not just for drying dishes. A damp tea towel folded over and placed under your mixing bowl is invaluable for keeping it in place, especially if you are using an electric hand mixer.
A damp tea towel is also great for placing over a bowl to protect dough when waiting for it to rise. Just resist all temptation to use it as an oven glove.

rolling pin
While I have been known to use an empty wine bottle for this purpose, I would advise buying a good solid one, whether wood, ceramic or glass. Make sure it is comfortable to hold and always wash after use.

measuring jug
Go for a glass one with all types of measurements clearly written on the side.

grater
Great for grating lemon and orange zest and also cheese and chocolate and all sorts of gorgeous goodies.

electrical equipment
I have whizzed up a few recipes in this book using my processor and used my good old hand held mixer for cake batters now and then, but if you don't have these items you are not hindered in any way. People were baking long before the advent of the blender and processor, so don't ever use that as an excuse not to bake.

girdle
No this is not an item of underwear, this is the Scottish term for a griddle. If you don't have one just use a heavy based frying pan instead.

jelly bag
Used for straining the juice from fruit, you can use muslin or even tights instead. Anything that you can pour your cooked fruit mash into that will allow the juices to drip

tools and tips – top tips

Everyone has their own way of doing things, some are pretty universal and some more localised to specific things. Here are the tips that I'd recommend for working with this book.

measurements
Each recipe is listed in both metric and imperial, use one or the other, don't mix together in same recipe as they are never exact translations.

butter
I have used unsalted butter in all the recipes. If you only have slightly salted butter and there is salt in the recipe, just cut down on the salt a little.

eggs
Eggs used here are all free range and medium in size. Here is a little run down on egg sizing; Medium 53-63g, Large 63-73g. As you can see there is a 10g difference within the size margins. Don't use eggs straight from the fridge, bring them up to room temperature first.

yeast
Where I have used yeast in recipes it is the little 7g packets of fast acting yeast available from most supermarkets.

fruits
Wash fruit before use. I have used unwaxed citrus fruit in recipes that require zest. Don't panic if you can't get unwaxed fruit, simply scrub fruit thoroughly in soapy water and rinse well, this will remove the wax coating.

pastry tips
Some people claim that they have hot hands and are therefore no good at making pastry, while cool hands might help they are not essential, so no excuses there then.
Do use firm cold butter to start with.
Do use cold or iced water when called for and don't use too much, you don't want a sloppy wet dough.
Don't be over generous when flouring your work surface and rolling pin as you can end up changing the consistency of your dough by using too much.
Do handle your dough as little as possible.
Do wrap in clingfilm and chill in fridge for 30 minutes after making your dough.

when all's said and done

How do you know when your cakes and bakes are ready to remove from the oven?
For fruit cakes test readiness by inserting a thin clean skewer into the middle of the cake for 30 seconds. The skewer should come out clean with no bits of cake batter attached to it.
Sponge type cakes should be well risen and golden in colour. To test if they are cooked through gently press the centre with your fingertip. If it springs back and leaves no indent the cake is ready. It should also have shrunk away from the sides of the tin a little.
Small cakes and buns should be firm to the touch.

If you do have to put a cake back in the oven and are worried that it will get too brown on top, simply place a piece of folded baking paper on top to protect it from colouring any more.

Preservation

Setting point

This is the point at which a jelly or jam is of the right consistency to be ladled into sterilised jars. You can check the set by first putting a saucer or small plate into the freezer for 5 minutes to chill it completely. When your jam or jelly has been boiling for the required time carefully scoop out a teaspoonful of the liquid and drop it on to the chilled plate. Leave it for 5 minutes and then touch with your finger tip. The jam should have skinned over and wrinkle holding the new shape.

Sterilising

Jars and bottles should be sterilised before using for your preserves. You can do this either by putting them through a hot wash in your dishwasher, or by washing in hot soapy water, rinsing well and placing in a warm oven for half an hour.

words and notes for American readers

I've used metric and imperial measurements in this book and there is also a conversion chart showing cup measurements. Some words may be confusing though, so here I shall try to clarify a few for you..

Bannock	*flat round cakes*
Baking tray	*cookie sheet*
Bicarbonate of soda	*baking soda*
Biscuits	*crackers/cookies*
Cake mix	*cake batter*
Cornflour	*corn starch*
Demerara sugar	*light brown sugar*
Digestive biscuits	*graham crackers*
Double cream	*whipping cream*
Frying pan	*skillet*
Girdle	*griddle*
Glace cherries	*candied cherries*
Golden syrup	*light corn syrup*
Greaseproof paper	*vegetable parchment*
Grill	*broil*
Icing	*frosting*
Jam	*preserves*
Mixed spice	*allspice*
Plain flour	*all-purpose flour*
Prove	*rise*
Self-raising flour	*all-purpose flour sifted with baking powder*
Soft brown sugar	*light brown sugar*
Strong white flour	*unbleached white flour*
Sultanas	*seedless white raisins*

Breads & Bannocks

Bread may be the staff of life, but it was the humble bannock that fed the Scottish nation for a great many years. Unlike bread, bannock baking requires no oven, so even armies on the move could rustle up their 'daily bread' quite easily.

Bannocks are very similar in make up to oatcakes, but are lighter with a more bread like texture. Once tasted I'm sure bannocks will become part of your baking repertoire.

Here are four simple recipes for some of my favourite breads and bannocks.

A little like French croissants in flavour, these tasty breads hail from Aberdeen (often called Aberdeen Butteries) where the men of the fishing fleets needed a snack with high fat content to keep them warm when working all hours on the rough seas.

Today they are more at home on the breakfast table accompanied by a dab of jam or honey.

butterie rowies

25g/1oz fresh yeast

1 tablespoon sugar

425ml/15fl oz water (this should be lukewarm)

450g/1 lb strong white flour

¼ teaspoon salt

225g/9oz butter

110g/4oz lard

Preheat the oven to **200C/400F/Gas 6**

Grease and flour a baking tray.

Add the sugar and yeast to half of the warm water and stir. Set aside for 15 minutes until it goes frothy on top.

Sift the flour and salt into a large bowl and gradually add the yeast mixture. Mix to a dough using more of the warm water if you need to. Turn out on to a floured surface and knead the dough for about 10 minutes before returning it to the bowl and covering with a damp cloth and placing in a warm spot for about 45 minutes or until it has doubled in size.

Cream together the butter and lard until well combined. Remove the dough from the covered bowl knock out the air and knead again for a few minutes before rolling out into a large rectangular shape approximately 1cm thick. Take about a third of the fat mixture and place little dots of it over two thirds of the dough area. Then fold the dough into three rather like making three folds of a sheet of paper to put in an envelope.

Reroll the dough again to its original size and go through the same procedure again with another third of the fat mixture. Repeat for a final time and this time when you roll out the dough cut it into small squares, you should get about 16 of them. Fold in the edges and corners of the squares so that they are almost oval in shape and place on the greased baking tray. Press the centres lightly with your fingers. Cover with the damp tea towel and set aside again in a warm spot to prove for a further 45 minutes.

To create the perfect steamy baking atmosphere for them place a roasting tin half filled with boiling water on the floor of your oven. Remove the tea towel and bake the butteries for **15-20 minutes** or until nicely golden.

fife bannock

This is a plain bannock without any fruit to sweeten it, perfect to use just as you would any other bread. These are like the traditional Scottish bannock that requires no yeast so could be baked on a girdle or in the oven if you prefer.

165g/6oz **plain flour**
½ teaspoon **bicarbonate of soda**
¾ teaspoon **cream of tartar**
¼ teaspoon **sugar**
¼ teaspoon **salt**

115/4oz **medium oatmeal**
1 tablespoon **butter**
buttermilk or greek yogurt
as required

Preheat your oven to **180C/350F/Gas 4**

Lightly grease a baking tray.

Sift the flour, bicarbonate of soda, cream of tartar, salt and sugar into a large bowl and add the oatmeal. Rub in the butter and add as much of the buttermilk or Greek yogurt as required to make a dough.

Turn out on to a floured surface and knead briefly. Make it into a rough circular shape and press down until it is about 1cm thick all round. Cut into quarters and either bake on a hot girdle (or heavy based frying pan) until brown on underside, turn over and brown the other side. Or bake in the oven for about **15 minutes**.

Let it cool on a wire rack.

morning rolls

No Scottish breakfast is complete without a floury roll. Served warm from the oven they are just as good filled with fried egg and bacon as with melting butter and a good dollop of fruity jam.

450g/1lb **strong white flour**
1 teaspoon **salt**
1 teaspoon **sugar**
7g packet of **fast action yeast**

25g/1oz **butter**
265ml/10fl oz lukewarm **milk** and **water** mixed

Preheat the oven to **220C/425F/Gas 7**

Scatter flour on two baking sheets.

Sift all dry ingredients into a large bowl and lightly rub in the butter. Make a well in the centre and pour in the liquid bringing together to form a dough. Tip out on to a floured surface and knead for about 10 minutes.

Return it to the bowl, cover with a damp tea towel and leave in a warm spot for about 1 hour until it has doubled in size.

Turn it out and knock out the air and knead lightly before dividing into 10 equal pieces. Roll each to about 10cm rounds and set well apart on your floured baking trays. Cover again and set aside to prove for a further 15-20 minutes.

Uncover the rolls and press each with your finger tips in the centre to spread the air bubbles and prevent blistering while they are baking. Brush each one with a little milk and sprinkle with some flour. Bake for **approximately 15-20 minutes** or until lightly browned. Dust with a little more flour if desired.

Cool on a wire rack and serve warm.

selkirk bannock

This fruity loaf was made famous by its originator Robbie Douglas who produced his first bannocks from his small bakery in Selkirk in 1859. He used simple but high quality ingredients and no spices or additives to flavour the bannock.

The Selkirk Bannock is a very versatile bread that's not too sweet so you can eat it in a variety of ways with sweet or savoury toppings and with everything from a cup of tea to a bowl of soup.

150g/5oz **butter**
50g/2oz **caster sugar**
2 x 7g packets of **fast action yeast**
900g/2lb **strong white flour**
¼ teaspoon **salt**

500ml/18fl oz **semi skimmed milk** or half **milk** half **water**
450g/1lb **sultanas**
1 tablespoon **milk** mixed with **sugar** to glaze

Preheat your oven to **190C/350F/Gas 5**

Lightly grease a baking tray.

For best results have all your ingredients warm to start with. Cream together the butter and sugar and stir in the flour, yeast and salt, add enough of the milk to form a dough.

Tip out on to a floured surface and knead for 10 minutes. Return to the bowl and cover with a damp tea towel and set aside in a warm place until the dough has doubled in size. Turn it out on to your floured surface again and knead a little, add the sultanas. Shape into a flat round loaf about 23cm/9" in diameter and place on the prepared baking sheet.

Cover the dough again and set aside for a further 40 minutes.

Bake the bannock for **approximately 1 hour** and then glaze the top with the milk and sugar mixture. Pop back into the oven for **10-15 minutes** more. Cool on a wire rack. The bannock should sound hollow when you tap the underside of it.

easy bread

This is such a simple loaf to make, it is my store cupboard standby that has rescued me on many an occasion when at first glance the cupboard appeared to be bare!

450g/1lb plain flour
25g/1oz caster sugar
25g/1oz butter
2 teaspoons bicarbonate of soda
2 teaspoons cream of tartar
1 teaspoon salt
275ml/1/2 pint buttermilk/sour cream or plain yogurt

Preheat oven to 190C/375F/Gas 5
Grease and line a baking sheet

Sift all dry ingredients into a large bowl and then rub in the butter. Add the buttermilk a little at a time to form a dough. Knead a couple of times and turn out on to a floured surface. Break in half and form two rounds. Sprinkle with a little extra flour and pop into the oven for 35 – 40 minutes. It should be golden and sound hollow when tapped underneath. Cool, slice and eat!

Simply Scones

Sweet or savoury, wildly extravagant, or totally simple, scones are whatever you make of them.

The following recipes will take you from breakfast to supper, and all times in between.

basic scones

These scones really do prove that with just a few simple ingredients and a little knowledge you can rustle up true comfort food at a moment's notice.

225g/8oz **self raising flour**
1 tablespoon **caster sugar**
pinch of **salt**

90g/3oz chilled unsalted **butter** diced
1 **egg**
50ml/2fl oz **milk**

Preheat the oven to **200C/400F/Gas 6**

Line a baking tray with baking paper.

Sift the flour, salt and sugar into a large bowl. Now add the diced butter rubbing it in with just your finger tips to create a breadcrumb-like mixture.

In a separate bowl whisk the egg and milk together and then make a well in the centre of your dry mix and start pouring in the eggy milk. Stir until the ingredients all come together to form a soft dough, (more milk can be added if required) and then turn out the dough onto a floured surface. Knead once or twice just to bring it all together.

Roll out until it is about 3-4cm (1½ inches) thick. Using a round cookie cutter or small glass cut out your scones and place on the prepared try.

Bake for **approximately 12 minutes** or until golden.

Makes about 10 scones.

Serve warm with butter or be really traditional and serve with clotted cream and lashings of your own lovely jam.

cheesy herb scones

These are wonderful served warm with either plain butter or lovely homemade lemon zesty herb butter. If you cut them with a really small cookie cutter (about 2cm) you get these gorgeous little savoury bites that are just perfect as nibbles with drinks.

400g/14oz **plain flour**
3 teaspoons **baking powder**
pinch of **salt**
90g/3oz chilled unsalted **butter** diced
2 **eggs**
200ml/7fl oz **milk**

60g/2¼oz grated **cheddar cheese**
1 tablespoon finely snipped **chives**
or **thyme**
¼ teaspoon ground **paprika**
(smoked variety if possible)

Preheat the oven to **200C/400F/Gas 6**

Grease and line a baking tray.

Sift the flour, salt, baking powder and paprika into a large bowl. Now add the diced butter rubbing it in with just your finger tips to create a breadcrumb-like mixture.

In a separate bowl whisk the eggs and milk together and then make a well in the centre of your dry mix and start pouring in the eggy milk.

Now add the herbs, grated cheese and stir until the ingredients all come together and then turn the dough onto a floured surface. Knead once or twice just to bring it all together.

Roll out the dough and if you are making standard scones make it about 3-4cm (1¼ - 1½ inches) thick. For the mini cocktail sized scones roll out to about 1½-2cm (½ inch). Use cutters to create your scones and place on prepared tray.

Bake for **approximately 12 minutes** or until golden.

Makes about 15 scones or about 40 cocktail scones.

Serve warm with herb butter, or for the ultimate in luxury serve with Scottish smoked salmon and some sour cream.

drop scones/scotch pancakes

This is always a confusing one for people, what's the difference between a Scotch Pancake and a Drop Scone, well nothing really it's just different words for the same gorgeously sweet and simple snack.

120g/4½oz **plain flour**
1 teaspoon **cream of tartar**
1 teaspoon **bicarbonate of soda**
Pinch of **salt**

1 **egg**
25g/1oz **caster sugar**
125ml/4fl oz **milk**
25g/1oz **butter**

Sift the flour, sugar, salt, cream of tartar and bicarbonate of soda into a large bowl and make a little well in the centre where you add the egg and milk. Melt the butter over a low heat and add this to the bowl and stir together all the ingredients. Beat for about one minute to get a really smooth batter. Set aside for ten minutes to settle before you start to cook the pancakes.

Set your girdle (griddle) or if you don't happen to have one just use a heavy based frying pan on a medium heat and use a teaspoon of butter to grease the pan. Wipe off extra.

Drop a tablespoon of the batter on to the girdle and let it cook until it turns golden brown and little bubbles appear on the surface, then flip it over using a palette knife and cook the other side. Remove from the girdle and wrap in a folded tea towel to keep warm while to cook the remaining pancakes.

Serve these warm with butter and a sprinkling of sugar. Or add your favourite jam, honey or jelly.

Makes about 15 pancakes.

fruit scones

I like to make these as rustic looking as possible and sometimes don't even use a cookie cutter to shape them. I think the rugged look with the colourful fruit popping out looks beautiful.

225g/8oz **self raising flour**
1 tablespoon **caster sugar**
pinch of salt
90g/3oz chilled **butter** diced

1 **egg**
50ml 2fl oz **milk**
40g/1 ½oz **glace cherries**
40g/1 ½oz **sultanas**

Preheat the oven to **200C/400F/Gas 6**

Line a baking tray with baking paper.

Sift the flour, salt and sugar into a large bowl. Now add the diced butter rubbing it in with just your finger tips to create a breadcrumb-like mixture. Chop the cherries and add these and the sultanas to the bowl. Reserve a little of the milk for glazing later.

In a separate bowl whisk the egg and milk together and then make a well in the centre of your dry mix and start pouring in the eggy milk. Stir until the ingredients all come together to form a soft dough, (more milk can be added if required) and then turn out the dough onto a floured surface. Knead once or twice just to bring it all together.

Roll out until it is about 3-4cm (1½ inches) thick. Using a round cookie cutter or small glass cut out your scones and place on the prepared tray. Brush on the reserved milk to glaze.

Bake for **approximately 12 minutes** or until golden.

Makes about 10 scones.

Serve warm with butter.

soda scones

Simplicity is the name of the game here, with only 5 ingredients and a throw it all together system, these scones really are a great basic.

115g/4oz **plain flour**
½ teaspoon **bicarbonate of soda**
½ teaspoon **cream of tartar**

Pinch of **salt**
4-5 tablespoons **milk**

Sift all the dry ingredients into a bowl and make a little well in the centre. Slowly add the milk, stirring to form a workable dough.

Tip dough out on to a floured surface and roll into a circular shape about 1cm (½ inch) thick.

Cut the dough into quarters.

Bake these on a lightly greased girdle (griddle) or heavy based frying pan for about **5 minutes** on each side, or until lightly browned.

Traditionally, soda scones would be taken from the pan and allowed to cool only slightly before being served with butter and maybe some of your favourite jam or jelly.

Another way to serve them is when they are cold, top with some cheddar cheese and then place under a hot grill until the cheese is all bubbly and melted, delicious!

tattie scones

A.k.a. potato scones if you want to be posh about it. These were traditionally made from leftover potatoes, but really they are so good it is well worth boiling up a pan of potatoes to make them and store some in the freezer when a hearty breakfast is calling. They are best eaten hot and can be served with butter and sometimes like pancakes with sugar, syrup or honey or jam. Personally I like mine with a traditional cooked breakfast as a real Sunday morning treat.

225g/8oz cooked **potato**
½ teaspoon **salt**

25g/1oz **butter**
50g/2oz **plain flour**

If using leftover potatoes warm them first to make the mixing easier. Mash the potatoes and add in the butter and salt. Now start adding the flour until you have a workable dough.

Roll out on a floured surface until about 5mm thick. Cut out two circles approximately 22cm in diameter using a plate as your guide. Cut each round into quarters.

Prepare your girdle (griddle) or heavy based frying pan by either lightly greasing or scattering with a little flour if you prefer a drier effect.

Bake the tattie scones for about **5 minutes** or until browned on both sides.

treacle scones

These always make me think of winter and log fires, just the smell of them makes me feel all cosy and warm.

225g/8oz **self raising flour**
1 tablespoon **caster sugar**
pinch of **salt**
90g/3oz chilled **butter**
1 **egg**

4 tablespoons **milk**
1 teaspoon **ground ginger**
1 teaspoon **mixed spice**
1 tablespoon **treacle**

Preheat the oven to **200C/400F/Gas 6**

Line a baking tray with baking paper.

Sift the flour, salt and spices into a large bowl and make a little well shape in the centre. Gently heat the butter with the sugar and treacle and stir until all sugar has dissolved. Add the milk but reserve a little for glazing the scones prior to baking.

Let the hot mixture cool a little before adding the egg and then pour it into the well in your dry mix. Stir to combine and bring together as a soft dough and then turn out onto a floured surface. Knead once or twice just to bring it all together.

Roll out until it is about 3-4cm (1½ inches) thick. Using a round cookie cutter or small glass cut out your scones and place on the prepared tray. Brush on the reserved milk to glaze.

Bake for **approximately 12 minutes** or until golden brown.

Makes about 8 scones.

Serve warm with butter.

Scotland is a nation of tea drinkers and when I think of scones I think of tea, so what better than to marry the two together in this delicious recipe. I use standard tea bags for this but I've tried it with Earl Grey and green tea too and it is great however you like your cuppa!

tea scones

- 2 tea bags
- 125ml/4fl oz boiling water
- 200g/6½ oz plain flour
- 2 teaspoons baking powder
- ¼ teaspoon salt
- 50g/1½oz butter
- 50g/1½oz caster sugar
- Grated zest of 1 lemon

Preheat oven to 220C/425F/Gas 7. Grease and line a baking sheet.

Pour water on to tea bags and leave to cool completely. Remove the tea bags. Sift flour, baking soda and salt into a bowl and rub in the butter until you have a breadcrumb like mixture. Now add the sugar and the grated lemon zest and the cold tea a little at a time to form a soft dough. Tip out on a floured surface and roll to approximately 1cm thick. Cut out scones with cookie cutter and glaze with a little milk.

Bake for about 8 minutes and then cool on a wire rack.

Serve with butter, jam or marmalade. A real tea time treat.

A Piece of Cake

A piece of cake is a part of the whole,
it is all about friendship and sharing.

To say something is 'a piece of cake'
means that it is easily accomplished.

All of these cakes are easy to make
and perfect for sharing.

black bun

Traditionally eaten on Twelfth Night nowadays it is synonymous with Hogmanay (New Year's Eve) celebrations in Scotland. The cake is distinctive in its strange outer casing of pastry and this was originally created as a way of keeping the cake moist during cooking and would have been broken off and discarded before the cake was cut. Now the pastry is kept as a special feature of the cake. For me it was always a very grown up sort of cake. My mum would make it in the first week of December every year and set it aside to mature and be ready to make its appearance on Hogmanay as the bells tolled the midnight hour and first footers would be welcomed in. My brother and I would be allowed to stay up late and would wait in eager anticipation for this cake and the other gorgeous goodies my mum would have prepared for family and friends who had come to welcome the New Year in.

Don't be put off by the huge list of ingredients, it really comes together quite easily once you get going and is well worth the effort.

pastry casing
350g/12oz **plain flour**
¼ teaspoon **salt**
25g/1oz caster sugar
175g/6oz **butter**
6 tablespoons iced **water**

filling
450g/1lb **currants**
450g/1lb **raisins**
175g/6oz **candied mixed peel**
225g/8oz **chopped almonds**

225g/8oz **plain flour**
225g/8oz **soft brown sugar**
2 **eggs** beaten
1 teaspoon each of **ground ginger**, **allspice powder**, **grated nutmeg** and **cinnamon**
¼ teaspoon **ground black pepper**
1 teaspoon each of **cream of tartar** and **baking soda**
6 tablespoons **whisky** (or **brandy**)
milk to bind it together
egg yolk for glaze

Preheat the oven to **180C/350F/Gas 4**

Grease and line a 2lb (1kg) loaf tin.

This is a two part process so make the pastry first by sifting the dry ingredients into a large bowl and rubbing in the butter. It is best to chop the butter into tiny pieces and rub in with just the finger tips. Add iced water to form a stiff dough. Wrap in clingfilm and chill for 30 minutes. Flour your work surface and roll the pastry thinly. Press this into the tin ensuring it is evenly distributed, make sure that you have enough left over to make the lid for the top!

Now on to stage 2, the easy bit; to make the cake filling simply put all the dry ingredients into a large bowl and mix thoroughly, stir in the eggs and whisky and add enough milk to bind it all together.

Pack it into the pastry case and level off the top. Cover with the remaining pastry to form a lid and seal all edges firmly together. Prick all over with a fork and brush with the egg yolk to glaze.

Bake for **2 hours** at the full heat and then reduce the oven temperature to **140C/275F/Gas 1** and bake for a further **1 hour** until the top is golden.

Let it cool before turning out of the tin.

NOTE; for a really festive look you can spray the outside casing with edible gold spray.

bramble berry bake

Brambles (or blackberries) grow prolifically in the Scottish countryside and no summer should be complete without a major bramble picking expedition. You can never seem to get enough into the basket without cramming in mouthfuls of these delicious fruits. Only thing is there is always that telltale purple lipstick look to give the game away!

This cake is simplicity itself but is so buttery and rich that it needs no accompaniment other than a good cuppa.

225g/8oz **butter** chopped
115g/4oz **caster sugar**
2 **eggs**
450g/1lb **plain flour**
½ teaspoon **baking powder**

¼ teaspoon **bicarbonate soda**
79ml/2½fl oz **milk**
200g/7oz **brambles**
Icing sugar to dust

Preheat the oven to **180C/350F**

Grease and line an 18cm spring form cake tin.

Beat the butter and sugar until pale and creamy and add the eggs a little at a time. Sift the flour, baking powder and bicarbonate of soda and add to the bowl. Beat in the milk. Gently fold in the brambles so that you don't break them too much.

Spoon the batter into the prepared tin and bake for **approximately 35 minutes** or until the cake is golden and a skewer comes out cleanly.

Cool on a wire rack.

cranachan cheesecake

For me cheesecake is comfort food at its best, especially a rich baked cheesecake full of texture and flavour, this one ticks all the boxes and is fancy enough to hold its own at any dinner party.

Note; if you can't get Crowdie (a soft Scottish cheese) just use cream cheese instead.

for the base
200g/6oz **shortbread** (preferably homemade)
50g/2oz medium **oatmeal**
50g/2oz melted **butter**

cheesecake filling
300g/10oz **cream cheese**
150g/5oz **Crowdie cheese**
125ml/4fl oz **sour cream**
5 **eggs**
200g/6oz **caster sugar**
30 **raspberries**

topping
200g/6oz **raspberries**
75g/2½oz **caster sugar**
1 tablespoon **water**

to serve
whipping cream
2 tablespoons **honey**
1 tablespoon **whisky**

Preheat the oven to **170C/325F/Gas 3**

Use a springform cake tin and line with paper and lightly grease.

Whizz up the base ingredients in a food processor until it comes together in a sandy clump. Press this into your prepared cake tin making sure you get it right into the edges and up the side of the tin, try to get an even layer about 2mm thick. Put in the fridge to harden while you make the filling.

Beat together the cream cheese and Crowdie along with the sugar. Add the eggs one at a time and continue beating (you can use your electric mixer) as you add the sour cream. Pour the mixture into the chilled base and then push in the raspberries all over the pie. Keep some on the surface and push other under the filling.

Place the cake tin into a larger baking tin and pour in boiling water into the outer tin to about half way up the sides of your cake tin. This *Bain Marie* will help the cheesecake come out really velvety and smooth. Bake for **1 hour** or until the top is golden but still has a bit of a wobble. Switch off oven and open the door and let the cake cool for an hour.

Keep it in its tin and set aside in the fridge overnight if possible to really let the flavours develop.

Remove from fridge at least an hour before serving and take it out of the tin.

Heat the raspberries and sugar until the sugar dissolves completely. Cool and pour over the cheesecake.

Serve with whipped cream with 1 tablespoon whisky and 2 tablespoons of honey whipped in.

dundee cake

King of the tea table, this rich moist fruit cake was once reserved only for special occasions like birthdays, christenings and maybe even Christmas. Never iced in any way, it is always presented with blanched almonds baked into the top, proof that style, taste and simplicity never go out of style.

400g/14oz **mixed dried fruit**
50g/2oz **ground almonds**
150g/5oz **butter**
150g/5oz **golden caster sugar**
Grated zest of a **lemon**

3 **eggs** beaten
115g/4oz **plain flour**
2 tablespoons **brandy**
50g/2oz **whole blanched almonds**

Preheat oven to **180C/350F/Gas 4**

Grease and line a deep 18cm/7inch round tin (spring form is best).

Mix together the dried fruit, ground almonds, lemon zest and brandy and set aside.

Cream together the butter and sugar and then add in the eggs a little at a time. Sift the flour and gradually fold this into the mix and then add the fruit mixture. Spoon into your prepared tin and level out. Make a slight dip in the centre of the cake. Now decorate with the whole almonds. You can do these in the traditional style starting with one in the centre and making larger and larger circles radiating out from there, or just dot them about as you please.

Bake for **1 hour** and then reduce the heat to **50C/300F/Gas 2** and bake for **another hour** or until a skewer pushed into the centre of the cake comes out clean. Leave to cool in the tin for 20 minutes before removing and cooling completely on a wire rack. Wrap in foil in an airtight container for a week before use to really improve the flavour. It will keep wrapped like this for up to three months if you can bear to wait that long…

glamis cake

This delightful date and walnut cake is named after Glamis Castle, the birthplace of HRH The Queen Mother. It's rich and fruity and really wonderful when spread with butter.

300g/7oz **pitted dates**
1 teaspoon **bicarbonate of soda**
250ml/8fl oz boiling **water**
2 **eggs**
200g/6oz **sugar**
25g/1oz **butter**

1 teaspoon **vanilla extract**
245g/8oz **plain flour**
1 teaspoon **salt**
2 teaspoons **baking powder**
200g/6oz **walnuts chopped**

Preheat the oven to **180C/350F/Gas 4**

Grease and line 9 x 12 inch baking tin.

Chop the dates and mix together with the bicarbonate of soda and boiling water. In a separate bowl beat together the eggs, sugar and butter until fluffy and add the vanilla extract and then the prepared dates.

Sift the flour, salt and baking soda into the mixture and add the nuts. Stir well to combine and then spoon into the prepared tin and bake for **approximately 45 minutes** or until a skewer comes out cleanly when pushed into the centre.

Leave in the tin for 5 minutes before removing and cooling on a wire rack. Make sure loaf is completely cold before cutting.

marmalade cake

As easy as summer sunshine. You can even use your own homemade whisky and ginger marmalade for a really grown up treat.

115g/4oz **butter** – softened
90g/3oz **light brown sugar**
2 **eggs**
225g/8oz **self raising flour**
½ teaspoon **baking powder**
Pinch of **salt**
Grated zest of an **orange**
3 tablespoons **marmalade**

3 tablespoons **milk**

topping
1 tablespoon **marmalade**
Juice of 1 **orange**
Grated zest of 1 **orange**
Icing sugar

Preheat oven to **180C/350F/Gas 4**

Grease a 1lb loaf tin or approx 20cm round cake tin.

Cream together the butter and sugar until fluffy. Beat the eggs and add these a little at a time. Sift the flour, salt and baking powder and add in just one table spoon at a time to get your mixture to start coming together. You can then fold in the rest of the flour etc. Stir in the orange zest, milk and marmalade and make sure everything is really well combined.

Spoon into your prepared tin and bake for **approximately 55-60 minutes**, or until a skewer comes out clean when pushed into the centre of the cake.

Let it cool for five minutes before easing out of the tin with a palate knife and let it cool completely on a wire rack.

Melt the marmalade and spread this thinly over the top of the cake and then make up your orange glaze as follows.

Grate the zest off the orange and set aside while you squeeze the juice into a bowl. Add enough icing sugar to make a pourable mix and drizzle this over the cake letting it run down the sides. Scatter the grated zest as a final flourish.

scottish tea loaf

When is a tea loaf essentially Scottish? When the dried fruits are soaked in whisky and tea of course! This fruit loaf is a great standby for afternoon tea or an evening snack.

450g/1lb **mixed dried fruits**
250g/9oz **soft light brown sugar**
200ml/7fl oz cold **tea**
2 teaspoons **Scotch whisky**

450g/1lb **self raising flour**
1 teaspoon **mixed spice**
1 **egg** beaten

This is a 2 part cake and you need to start things off the night before you want to bake it.

Mix together the dried fruit and sugar and pour over the cold tea and whisky (whisky is optional you can go for just straight tea if you prefer, but it does give a lovely depth of flavour), cover the bowl and leave to soak overnight.

Preheat the oven to **190C/375F/Gas 5**

Line a 2lb loaf tin with greased baking paper.

Uncover your bowl and you will find that the fruit is beautifully swollen and juicy now. Sift the flour and spice into the fruit and stir well to combine. Now add the beaten egg and mix it all thoroughly.

Spoon the mixture into the prepared tin and bake for **approximately 50 minutes**, or until a skewer comes out clean when pushed into the centre. If the cake is browning on top too much just put a piece of folded baking paper on top to protect it.

Let the cake cool in its tin for about 5 minutes and then take it out and let it cool thoroughly on a wire rack.

seed cake

A classic cake that has graced many a tea table down the years. It is flavoured with caraway seeds which make an appearance in quite a few Scottish bakes. I like the addition of the citrus zest, but if you want a plainer cake just leave that out.

175g/6oz **self raising flour**
175g/6oz **butter**
175g/6oz **sugar**
3 **eggs**

25g/1oz **ground almonds**
1 tablespoon **caraway seeds**
Grated zest of half an **orange**
Grated zest of half a **lemon**

Preheat oven to **180C/350F/Gas 4**

Grease and line an 18cm/7inch cake tin.

Cream together the butter and sugar until fluffy and then beat in the eggs and add the almonds, caraway seeds and the grated citrus zest. Now stir in the flour and make sure everything is well combined.

Pour into the prepared tin and bake for **approximately 40 minutes** or until golden on top and a skewer comes out cleanly.

Let it cool for about 5 minutes then remove from the tin and cool completely on a wire rack.

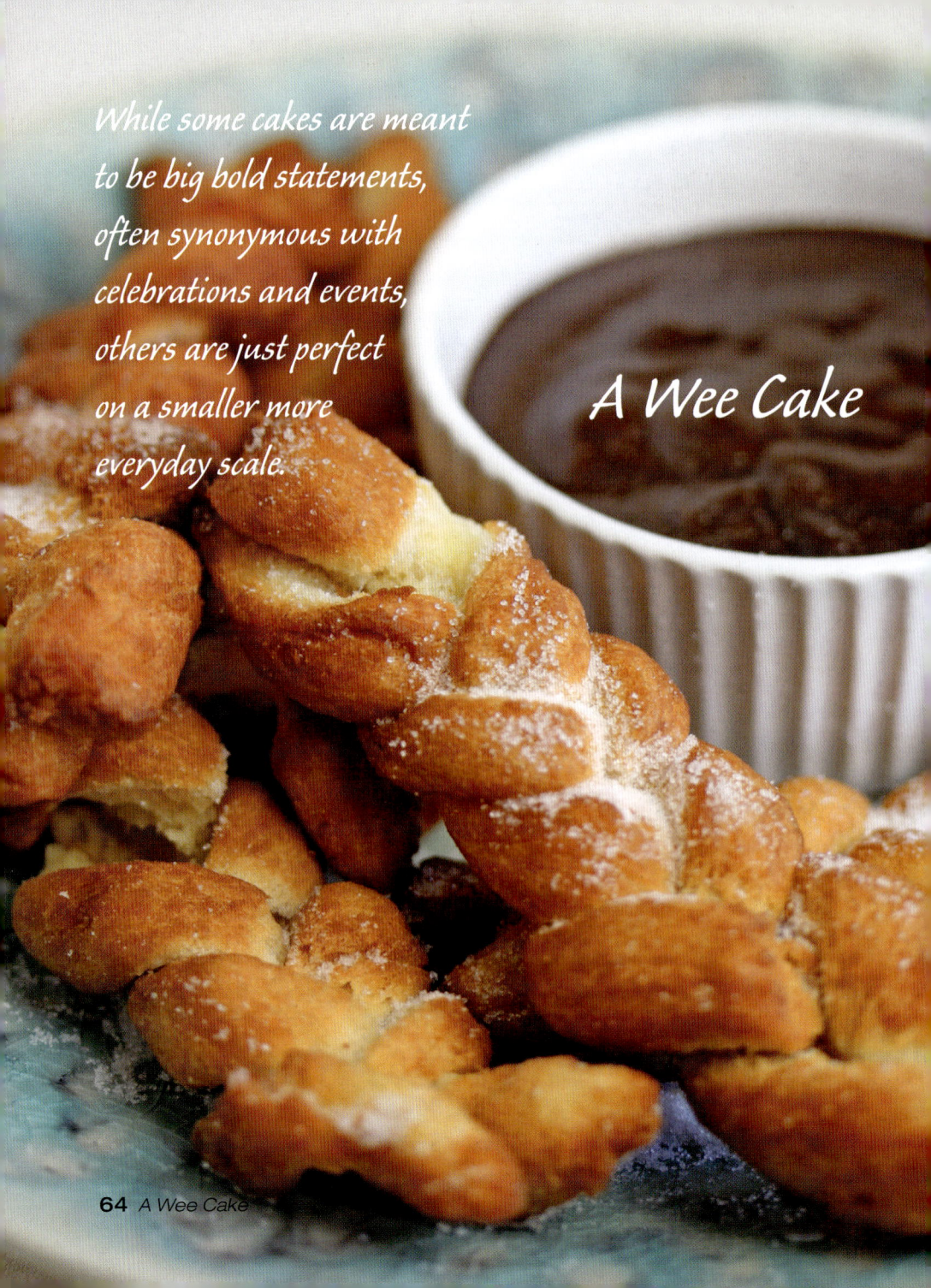

While some cakes are meant to be big bold statements, often synonymous with celebrations and events, others are just perfect on a smaller more everyday scale.

A Wee Cake

crulla

This is definitely one for those with a sweet tooth. These sugary plaits are mainly associated with Aberdeen and thought to derive from the doughnuts brought into Scotland by the Dutch fishing fleets. Kids love these, but for an adult treat I like to serve them with my whisky and chocolate dip, yummy!

50g/2oz **butter**
50g/2oz **caster sugar**
1 **egg**
225g/8oz **self raising flour**
¼ teaspoon **salt**
½ teaspoon **ground ginger**

1 tablespoon **buttermilk** or **greek yogurt**
oil for frying
icing sugar to dust

Cream the butter and sugar until light and fluffy. Beat the egg and add a little at a time. Sift the flour, salt and ginger into the mixture and combine. Add the buttermilk or Greek yogurt to make a fairly stiff dough.

Pull the dough into pieces and roll into long thing strings about the size and length of a pencil. Take 3 of these pieces and pinch together the top and then plait/braid the 3 strands together. Pinch the end together to stop it unravelling. Do this with all the dough. This is a great job for children to help with.

Heat the oil (use something unflavoured like vegetable oil for this) in a deep pan and carefully drop in the crulla 2 at a time. Fry for **2-3 minutes** each side till golden. Remove with slotted spoon and dry on kitchen paper. Dust with a little icing sugar to serve.

honey buns

These honey flavoured buns are light, sweet and very moreish indeed!

3 tablespoons **honey**
50g/2oz **sugar**
50g/2oz **butter**
115g/4oz **plain flour**
½ teaspoon **bicarbonate of soda**
25g/1oz chopped **walnuts**
25g/1oz ground **almonds**

grated zest of ½ **orange**
1 **egg** beaten

for the topping
230g/8oz **icing sugar**
2-3 tablespoons **cream cheese**
6 **walnut halves** to decorate

Preheat the oven to **180C/350F/Gas 4**

Place cupcake liners in a 6 hole muffin tin.

Gently heat the sugar, honey and butter in a small pan until the sugar has completely dissolved. Let this cool for 5 minutes.

Sift the flour and bicarbonate of soda into a large bowl and add the chopped walnuts, ground almonds and orange zest.

Add the beaten egg to the melted sugar mix and slowly pour this into the dry ingredients and stir well to combine.

Spoon it into the lined muffin tins until each is about 2/3rds full. Bake for **approximately 15 minutes** or until puffy and deep golden brown in colour.

Let them rest for about 5 minutes in the tin before tipping out on to a wire rack to cool thoroughly.

To make the topping; sift the icing sugar into a bowl and add the cream cheese one tablespoon at a time beating well. You may only require 2 tablespoons of the cream cheese depending on the consistency of icing that you like. Spoon this on top of each bun and top with half a walnut.

A Wee Cake

montrose cakes

These delightful little mouthfuls have the delicate flavour of rose and the spice of nutmeg, a heady combination indeed.

80g **unsalted butter**
75g **sugar**
2 **eggs**
45g **currants**

2 tablespoons **brandy**
2 teaspoons **rose water**
70g **self raising flour**
¼ teaspoon grated **nutmeg**

Preheat the oven to **190C/375F/Gas 5**

Grease a large tart tin or 2 nine hole tins.

Cream together the butter and sugar until light and fluffy. Beat the eggs and add a little at a time until well combined. Stir in the currants, brandy and rose water. Sift the flour and nutmeg together and add these to the butter mixture stirring well.

Spoon the mixture into the prepared tart tins making sure that each well is no more than half full.

Bake for **approximately 10 minutes** or until the edges are just browned.

Allow to cool for about 5 minutes before tipping on to a wire rack to cool completely.

Makes approximately 18 little cakes

porridge pancakes

I love these, to me they are the ultimate in breakfast food and easy enough to make any day of the week. Add a few fresh berries and a little honey and your day will be off to a fabulous start.

150g/5oz **plain flour**
1 teaspoon **baking powder**
½ teaspoon **bicarbonate of soda**
½ teaspoon **salt**
60g/2oz **soft brown sugar**

25g/1oz **quick cook porridge oats**
1 **egg**
237ml/8fl oz **milk**
25g/1oz **butter**

Sift flour, baking powder, bicarbonate of soda and salt into a bowl and stir in the porridge oats and sugar. Melt the butter and beat this with the egg and milk in a separate bowl. Pour into the dry ingredients and mix well until thoroughly blended.

Lightly grease a girdle (griddle) or heavy based frying pan and place on a medium heat. Spoon about 2 tablespoons of the batter per pancake on to the girdle.

Little bubbles will appear on the tops just as they are ready to flip over. Cook until nicely golden brown on both sides.

Serve warm with honey, syrup, jam or jelly and a good dollop of butter. Sheer bliss and a great way to start the day!

sair heidies

This amazing name translates as 'sore heads' and comes from the fact that these simple little sponge cakes are made with a paper wrapper around them to signify a bandage and the muffin shaped top is crusted with crumbled lump sugar like broken aspirin tablets – the image of a very sore head indeed.

In the north of Scotland where these originate they use special round rings to create them, I used those metal presentation rings that you get for making stacked up veggies etc.

140g/5oz **self raising flour**
50g/2oz **butter**
50g/2oz **caster sugar**

2 **eggs**
4 **sugar lumps** crushed

Preheat the oven to **200C/400F/Gas 6**

Greased and lined baking tray plus metal presentation rings (or a muffin tray).

Cut out 6 strips of baking paper about 4cm x 15cm (depending on the size of your metal rings or width of the muffin trays. Line the rings or muffin trays with the paper, overlapping the end so there are no gaps.

Sift the flour and sugar into bowl and beat in the butter and eggs until light and fluffy.

Spoon into the lined metal rings or the muffin tins.

Place the sugar lumps on a piece of kitchen roll and fold over (this is to stop the sugar flying everywhere) now give it a whack with your rolling pin but don't overdo it as you want little chunks of sugar, not dust! Scatter this on top of the cakes.

Bake for about **15 minutes** then cool on a wire rack.

I added a string tie just to finish them off.

scottish snowballs

Almost like a cross between a scone and shortbread with a jammy filling and of course icing and coconut 'snow' all over, yummy!

225g/8oz **self raising flour**
90g/3oz **caster sugar**
¼ teaspoon **salt**
90g/3oz **butter**
1 **egg**

1 **egg yolk** only
180g/6oz **icing sugar**
Jam
50g/2oz **desiccated coconut**

Preheat oven to **200C/400F/Gas 6**

Grease and line a baking tray.

Sift flour, salt and sugar into a bowl and rub in the butter till you get a breadcrumb-like mixture. Slowly mix in the egg and extra yolk. Bring together to form a dough and add a little extra flour if it is too loose to work with.

Break into two balls and then into half again. Now make five little balls out of each quarter of the original dough. You should end up with 20 small balls about half the size of a golf ball.

Bake on a greased tray for **approximately 15 minutes** until golden. Set aside on a wire rack to cool completely.

Meanwhile dig out your favourite jam to sandwich them together in pairs.

Have two small bowls ready and in one add about two tablespoons of water to the icing sugar to make a thin icing. You only want to dip the snowballs into this and use it as glue to attach the coconut, if the icing is too thick it will make the task really messy and almost impossible.

In the other bowl have the desiccated coconut and roll the iced balls in this. Now pop them on a plate to set before everyone gobbles them all up.

What A Tart

Like the perfect gift wrapped in delicious pastry.

almond flory

This sweet and fancy latticed tart was very popular in Edinburgh's finest tea rooms. I have used half cream and half *fromage frais* to cut down on the fat content, feel free to use all cream if you prefer.

1 pkt **frozen puff pastry**

filling
50g/2oz **butter**
115g/4oz **soft brown sugar**
1 **egg**
1 **egg yolk** only
40ml/1½ fl oz **cream**

40ml/1½fl oz **fromage frais**
1 tablespoon **brandy**
1 teaspoon **orange flower water**
115g/4oz **ground almonds**
115g/4oz **mixed dried fruit**
¼ teaspoon ground **cinnamon**
¼ teaspoon ground **nutmeg**
grated zest of 1 **lemon**

Preheat oven to **220C/425F/Gas 7**

Lightly grease a loose base 22cm/10" flan tin.

Roll out pastry as thin as possible and press into the flan tin. Reserve all the extra pastry for making the latticed top.

Cream together the butter and sugar until fluffy. Beat the egg and extra egg yolk and add these slowly. Now gradually add the cream and *fromage frais*. Add all other ingredients and stir well. Pour this into the pastry case and smooth it around.

Roll out the remaining pastry and cut into strips to make a latticed top for the pie and pinch the edges into the base to secure. Glaze with a little milk before baking for **approximately 35 minutes** or until golden. Remove from oven and sprinkle with sugar, allow to cool in the tin for 10 minutes.

auld alliance appley tart

A criss cross of Scotland and France here with the simplest ever open faced apple pie. I've used bought puff pastry for ease but if you feel the urge make your own.

350g/12oz **puff pastry**
4 eating **apples**
Juice and zest of 1 whole **lemon**
4 teaspoons **golden granulated sugar**

25g/1oz **butter**
2 tablespoons Scottish heather **honey** (any honey will do though)

Preheat oven to **220C/425F/Gas 7**

Grease and line a baking tray.

Zest the lemon and then squeeze out all juice and keep this in a bowl ready to dip the apples. Peel and core the apples and cut into quarters. Thinly slice the apples evenly so that no areas are thicker than the other. Roll all the apple slices in the lemon and zest mix and leave them ready for use in the bowl.

Roll out the puff pastry on a floured surface till it is about 2mm thick. Cut out four circles approximately 15cm in diameter, I used an upturned soup bowl as my guide for this.

Place the rounds on a greased baking sheet spaced well apart and now start adding the apple slices. You want to create an even circle with each slice overlapping the next. Once all the rounds are covered in apple slices sprinkle them with the golden caster sugar and dot with small pieces of butter.

Bake for **approximately 15-20 minutes** or until puffed up and golden.

Serve these warm from the oven, and, as a finishing touch warm up the honey and drizzle it over the pies as a gorgeous glaze.

border tart

The Scottish border region boasts many recipes and this rich fruity tart is one of the finest.

pastry base
175g/6oz **plain flour**
90g/3oz **butter**
25g/1oz **caster sugar**
1 **egg** (yolk only)

filling
1 **egg**
75g/3oz **soft brown sugar**
50g/2oz **butter**
2 teaspoons **white wine vinegar**
115g/4oz **currants**
25g/1oz **walnuts** – chopped

Preheat the oven to **190C/375F/Gas 5**

Grease and line a 20cm (8") flan tin.

Make the pastry case first by sifting the flour into a bowl and gently rubbing in the butter with your fingertips, now add the sugar and use the egg yolk to bring it all together.

Turn out on to floured surface and roll thinly to about 2mm thick. Use your rolling pin to help lift the pasty on to the flan tin and press into the tin and up the sides. Trim off excess pastry from edges. Set aside while you make the filling.

Melt the butter over a gentle heat and then pour this into a large bowl with the egg and sugar, mix well. Now add the other ingredients and stir to combine.

Pour the filling into the prepared pastry case and give it a shake to level it all out. Bake for **approximately 30 minutes** or until pastry is golden.

Remove from oven and allow to cool in the tin for at least 10 minutes and then cool a little more on a wire rack before serving warm with a dollop of whipped cream.

bramble and apple frushie

Frushie is an old Scots word meaning crumble and this pastry has a lovely crumbly texture. Traditionally apples are used as the filling, but you can really use any fruit you like.

for the pastry
200g/7oz **plain flour**
Pinch of **salt**
50g/2oz **butter**
50g/oz **lard**
1 **egg** yolk only

fruit filling
115g/4oz **apples**
115g/4oz **brambles** (blackberries)
50g/2oz **clear honey**

Preheat oven to **200C/400F/Gas6**

Grease a 23cm pie dish.

To make the pastry. Sift the flour into a bowl and add the salt. Rub in the butter and lard till the mixture is like fine breadcrumbs. Add the egg yolk and mix to a stiff dough. Let it rest in the fridge for about half an hour.

Roll out the pastry and press into the pie dish, cut off excess pastry and roll into strips for the top of the tart. Peel and slice the apples very thinly. Lay them on the base of the tart. Scatter on the brambles and pour the honey evenly over the fruit. Lay the strips of pastry in a lattice pattern on top and seal the edges with a little water.

Bake in a hot oven for **25-30 minutes**. Sprinkle with caster sugar and serve with cream or ice cream. Enjoy.

Just Ginger

With everything from sticky cake to crunchy biscuits going under the gingerbread banner, you could be forgiven for thinking that some things must be incorrectly named. Not so, the first gingerbreads were hard and biscuit-like being made from stale crumbs and spices. Over the centuries they have adapted with the advancements in raising agents and become more and more cake like. So gingerbread really is all things to all men.

ginger jacks

A.k.a. sticky fingers! These were always our favourites as kids, so sweet, so tempting, you never could keep your fingers out of the cookie jar when these guys were around.

350g/12oz **butter**
275g/10oz **caster sugar**
225g/8oz **golden syrup**
450g/1lb **medium oatmeal/porridge oats**

1 tablespoon **ground ginger**
Grated zest of an **orange**

Preheat oven to **180C/350F/Gas 4**

Grease and line 28 x 18cm/11 x 7in shallow tin.

Melt the butter, sugar and syrup in a large pan over low heat. When all the sugar has dissolved add the ginger and the grated zest of the orange and stir in the oats. Make sure everything is well mixed and pour out into your prepared tin.

Bake for **approximately 35 minutes** or until golden around the edges.

Leave to cool in the tin for 15 minutes or so and while it is still warm score into squares or fingers.

When it is completely cold remove from tin and cut the pieces through.

I like to drizzle mine with a little squiggle of icing, things can never be too sweet can they!

broonie

This style of gingerbread hales from Orkney although it is very similar to Parkin known in lowland Scotland and the north of England. Strangely enough Broonie is not named after its brown (or broon in Scotland) colouring but comes instead from the old Norse word *Bruni* meaning a thick bannock.

175g/6oz **plain flour**
Pinch of **salt**
1 teaspoon **baking powder**
115g/4oz **soft brown sugar**
2 teaspoons **ground ginger**

175g/6oz medium **oatmeal**
2 tablespoons **butter**
2 tablespoons **treacle**
1 **egg**
270ml/10fl oz **buttermilk**

Preheat the oven to **180C/350F/Gas 4**

Grease and line a 2lb (900g) loaf tin.

Sift the flour, ginger, salt and baking powder into the oatmeal. Rub in the butter until you have a breadcrumb-like mixture. Melt the treacle over a low heat and stir in the egg and most of the buttermilk. Add this a little at a time to the oaty mixture and stir to form a soft dough that drops off the spoon.

Pour into your prepared tin and bake for **1¼ hours** until well risen or a skewer comes out clean when pushed into the centre.

Leave in the tin for 5 minutes before removing and cooling on a wire rack. It is best to leave this until it is completely cold before you cut it.

This type of gingerbread tastes best if you keep it wrapped in foil or in an airtight tin for a week to let the flavours mature before eating it.

edinburgh gingerbread

Edinburgh was always the centre of high society in Scotland and led the field in fashion and innovation. This was very true in the food department where Edinburgh hostesses would boast the latest spices and ingredients in their cakes and bakes. This distinctive gingerbread is no exception and has cinnamon for added spice and the crunch of almonds as well as juicy sultanas.

225g/8oz **plain flour**
1 teaspoon **bicarbonate of soda**
2 teaspoons ground **ginger**
1 teaspoon **cinnamon**
Pinch of **salt**
175g/6oz **butter**

12 tablespoons **treacle**
110g/4oz **soft brown sugar**
6 tablespoons **milk**
2 **eggs**
50g/2oz **sultanas**
50g/2oz **flaked almonds**

Preheat oven to **160C/325F/Gas 3**

Grease and line a 2lb (1 kilo) loaf tin.

Sift together the flour, spices, salt and bicarbonate of soda and add the nuts and fruit. Melt the butter, treacle and sugar together over a low heat until the sugar has completely dissolved, let this cool slightly before adding the eggs and milk and stirring well. Add this a little at a time to the dry ingredients and mix well.

Pour the mixture into your prepared tin and bake for approximately **1¼ hours**.

gingerbread husbands

Oh yes, this is what the humble gingerbread man used to be called in Scotland many years ago!

Whether you make these in the traditional 'husband' shape with proper currant eyes and buttons and a cherry grin, or choose to go for modern hearts with icing on top, gingerbread shapes are always popular and not just at Christmas.

125g/4oz **butter**
125g/4oz **dark brown sugar**
3 tablespoons **golden syrup**
1 tablespoon **treacle**
300g/10oz **plain flour**

1 teaspoon **bicarbonate of soda**
2 teaspoons **ground ginger**
2 teaspoons **mixed spice**
currants and **glace cherries** to decorate

Preheat oven to **180C/350F/Gas 4**

Grease and line 2 baking sheets.

In a heavy based pan melt the butter with the treacle, golden syrup, sugar. Stir in the flour, bicarbonate of soda and spices until the mixtures forms a soft, thick dough. Gather into a ball and wrap in clingfilm and chill for 30 minutes until firm.

Lightly flour your work surface and roll out the dough to about 2-3cm thick and use a cookie cutter to cut out your 'husbands' (hearts or whatever else you fancy). Half the currants and use as eyes and buttons and carefully cut slithers of glace cherry to make his cheeky grin. Use a palate knife to lift them on to your prepped sheets and bake for **approximately 10 minutes** until golden and firm, be careful not to overcook them or they will turn into rock. Cool on a rack.

Makes about 16 depending on size of husbands of course!

gingernuts

Gingernuts bring back two memories for me; my mum dunking one in her tea and always managing to whip it out before the biscuit dissolved (a feat I could never seem to manage and always ended up with a sweetie soup mix!) and a daft game we kids would play where you held the Gingernut in your right palm and had to break it with your left elbow. The person with the most pieces was the winner.

I've made my Gingernuts extra large as I think they should be a whole snack in themselves.

350g/12oz **self raising flour**
Pinch of **salt**
200g/7oz **caster sugar**
1 tablespoon **ground ginger**
1 teaspoon **bicarbonate of soda**

1 teaspoon **grated orange rind**
125g/4½oz **butter**
5 tablespoons **golden syrup**
1 **egg** beaten
Caster sugar to sprinkle

Preheat oven to **160C/325F/Gas 3**

Grease and line a baking tray.

Sift together all the dry ingredients into a big bowl so you have plenty of room to work the dough as it forms.

Heat the golden syrup with butter to melt and let this cool slightly before adding to the dry ingredients so as not to burn yourself when you start to bring things together. Add the egg and mix to form a dough.

Pull off pieces and roll into balls (mine were about the size of golf balls) and space these well apart on a baking tray. Lightly press to flatten slightly. Sprinkle with a little caster sugar prior to baking to get that crackled crazy paving look. Bake for **15-20 minutes** and then cool on a wire rack.

Makes about 20 big biscuits but you can be more delicate in the sizing and have lots more.

parlies

These spicy little biscuits were originally called Edinburgh Parliament Biscuits due to their popularity in government circles many years ago. A very simple little biscuit, they would have been square in shape, but I rather like the casual dollop-like look of these.

60g/2oz **caster sugar**
115g/4oz **butter**
225g/8oz **plain flour**

1 teaspoon **ground ginger**
1 **egg**
2 tablespoons **treacle**

Preheat the oven to **180C/350F/Gas 4**

Grease a large baking tray.

Cream the butter and sugar until fluffy. Warm the treacle slightly so that it blends more easily with the other ingredients and stir the egg into the treacle. Sift the flour with the ginger so it is well combined and then add this along with the eggy treacle a little at a time to your butter mix and blend well.

Drop teaspoonfuls of the batter on to your baking sheet spaced well apart as they will spread as they bake.

Pop into the oven for **approximately 15-20 minutes**.

Cool on a wire rack.

Specially Shortbread

The sweetness of Scotland

ayrshire shortbread

I live in Ayrshire so I have to be just a little bit biased on this one, Ayrshire shortbread is gorgeous! Our county is famed for its cows and dairy produce, so it is no surprise that our shortbread contains cream. It really is richer and more luxurious than the more basic shortbread so makes a real tea time treat.

200g/7oz **plain flour**
25g/1oz **cornflour**
115g/4oz **unsalted butter chopped**

115g/4oz **caster sugar**
1 **egg yolk**
2 tablespoons **cream**

Preheat oven to **150C/300F/Gas 2**

Grease and line a baking sheet.

Sift the flours into a bowl and rub in the butter to form a breadcrumb-like mixture. Stir in the sugar. In a cup whisk together the egg yolk and cream and then add this to your mixture. Bring everything together to form a dough but don't over work it.

Tip out onto a floured surface and roll out to about 5mm thick and cut with round cookie cutters. Or you can press it into a traditional wooden shortbread mould if you have one.

Bake for **approximately 15 minutes** until the shortbread is firm to the touch and has just a little colour.

Cool on a wire rack and sprinkle with a little sugar before serving.

millionaires shortbread

There is only one word for this – yum! You can buy this treat in any bakery but really it is so simple to make, tastes ten times better than the bought stuff and looks a million dollars.

base
115g/4oz **butter**
175g/6oz **plain flour**
55g/2oz **golden caster sugar**

toppings
175g/6oz **unsalted butter**
115g/4oz **golden caster sugar**
3 tablespoons **golden syrup**
400g/14oz canned **condensed milk**
200g/7oz good quality **chocolate** (70% cocoa solids) I used a mixture of milk and plain together and then swirled some white on top for decoration.

Preheat oven to **180C/350F/Gas 4**

Line a 23cm shallow baking tin.

You can do the shortbread base in a food processor for quickness if you like. Just whizz together all the base ingredients to bind and then roll out the dough to fit your baking tin.

Bake for **approximately 25 minutes** or until golden on top.

To make the filling heat up the butter, condensed milk, sugar and golden syrup in a pan and stir until the sugar has all dissolved. Now raise the temperature and bring to the boil and then simmer for about 8 minutes. Keep stirring so it doesn't stick to the pot. It should become lovely and thick. Pour this over the shortbread base and put it in the fridge to cool completely and become firm.

Melt the chocolate in a double boiler (bowl over pot of water without water touching underside of bowl) or in the microwave and spread this all over the caramel topped shortbread. Pop it back in the fridge to set completely and then cut out squares or fingers with a sharp knife.

As I said, yum!

petticoat tails

Anyone familiar with those round tartan tins of shortbread will recognise the delicate round shape of the famous Petticoat Tails shortbread. Rolled thinner than the basic shortbread fingers this mix contains milk so has a lightness about it that suits the more delicate look. It actually takes its name from the round and fluted shape of an Elizabethan petticoat skirt but stories abound that its name derived from the French *Petites Gatelles* meaning Little Cakes.

225g/8oz **plain flour**
60g/2oz **caster sugar**
115g/4oz **butter** (chopped)

2 tablespoons **milk**
Caraway seeds (optional)

Preheat oven **180C/350F/Gas 4**

Grease and line a baking tray.

Sieve together the flour and sugar and then rub in the butter. Add the caraway seeds if using and then the milk a little at a time to form a soft dough.

Tip your dough directly on to your baking tray and roll out to a mere 4mm thick (this is traditionally much finer than standard shortbread) and using a plate as your guide cut out a circle shape. Pinch around the edges with thumb and fore finger to get the petticoat edging and then use either a glass or a cookie cutter to cut a 2" circle in the centre and then divide the outer ring into eight pieces. Don't move them just make the cuts. Prick all over with a fork.

Place in the oven and bake for **approximately 30 minutes** until crisp and golden.

Cool and sprinkle with sugar.

shortbread sandwich

Mixing my two favourite things, jam and shortbread just has to be a winner, and this simple tray bake will have your friends and family clamouring for more.

115g/4oz softened **butter**
115g/4oz caster **sugar**
175g/6oz **plain flour**
½ teaspoon **baking powder**

1 **egg** lightly beaten
few drops of **vanilla extract**
Your favourite **jam**

Preheat oven to **17C/325F/Gas 3**

Line a 30x 40cm/12 x 16" baking tray.

Cream together the butter and sugar. Sift the flour and baking powder and add these a bit at a time. Now add the beaten egg and a few drops of vanilla extract and knead until you have a soft dough.

Wrap in cling film and chill for 30 minutes to firm up.

Flour your surface and after dividing the dough into two equal parts, roll the first to about 2mm thick and transfer this to your baking tray. Be a bit creative patchwork wise if you have to, to make it fit the tin. Smooth it out.

Now spoon on the jam as if you were being generous on hot toast. Make sure you cover the entire surface right to the edges.

Roll out the second ball of dough and lift this (use your rolling pin here) and place on top of the jam. You want it to cover the bottom layers completely.

Bake for **approximately 15-20 minutes** or until it is golden in places and starting to brown nicely at the edges.

Let it cool for about five minutes before lifting from the tin and cutting out either in plain squares or slices or get creative with the cookie cutters and go for jammy hearts (I couldn't resist). Leave to cool completely on a wire rack.

simple shortbread

There are so many different types of shortbread in Scotland and they are all wonderful in their own right. Everyone has their own special recipe that they absolutely swear by, this is mine for a really quick and easy shortbread that you can whip up at (almost) a moment's notice when friends pop round for tea. With only 4 ingredients you really can't go far wrong.

175g/6oz **plain flour**
Pinch of **salt**

60g/2oz **caster sugar**
115g/4oz **butter**

Preheat oven to **150C/300F/Gas 2**

Grease and line a baking tray.

Sieve the flour and salt into a bowl and stir in the sugar. Chop the butter into small pieces and toss this into the dry ingredients. Now simply rub it in with your fingers to create a dough. You can either press the dough into a round greased baking tin for a traditional disc, or roll it out to approximately 1½-2cm thick (for cutting into chunky fingers) or slightly thinner for cutting into rounds. If you are making shortbread fingers place the dough on a baking sheet as it is. Prick with a fork for decoration, and if using a baking tin pinch dough round the edges for a pretty effect.

Bake for **approximately 45-50 minutes** until the shortbread is firm to the touch and has just a little colour.

Cut into bars or quarters if using a round tin and leave to cool while still in the baking tin. Sprinkle with a little sugar and serve with tea.

strawberry shorties

Make sure you roll the shortbread base nice and thin for a real melt in the mouth experience. The Demerara sugar gives these a really amazing taste and superb crunch.

115g/4oz **self raising flour**
25g/1oz **plain flour**
115g/4oz **butter**
2 tablespoons **demerara sugar**
Pinch of **salt**

topping
6-10 tablespoons **mascarpone cheese**
icing sugar to taste
Few drops of **vanilla extract**
250g/8oz **strawberries** hulled and cut into halves
1 tablespoon **pistachio nuts** crushed

Preheat oven to **180C/350F/Gas 4**

Line a baking tray.

You can whizz this up in your food processor really easily so it is very quick to make. Start by mixing the flours and salt and then adding the butter. Finally add the sugar and bring it all together as a crumbly ball. Wrap in clingfilm and leave in the fridge for at least half an hour.

Cut the dough into 6 pieces and roll out on a floured surface to make a thin circle about 2mm thick and measuring approximately 10cm. I used a large cookie cutter to make life easier.

Place on an ungreased baking tray and pop into the oven for **10-15 minutes** until just golden and firm to touch, be careful not to over cook them as you don't want these beauties to be rock hard.

Beat the mascarpone with a few drops of vanilla extract and add icing sugar to taste. Cover each shortbread disc generously with the creamy mix and add the strawberry halves in any formation you fancy. Dust with a little icing sugar and scatter over the crushed pistachios. Makes 6.

Specially Shortbread 107

Taking The Biscuit

A wee selection of biscuits starting with those featuring that mainstay of Scotland, oats, then on to some that are just downright yummy!

easy oatcakes

No Scottish cook book would be complete without an oatcake recipe and this one is no exception. These simple biscuits have been a staple of the Scottish diet for centuries and traditionally used to be kept buried in oatmeal in a girnel or meal chest. However there is no need to go to such lengths nowadays, they keep beautifully in a tin. Don't just think of oatcakes as something to have with cheese, spread them with butter and jam, marmalade or honey, or have them with a warming bowl of soap on a chilly day. They are as versatile as bread and good for you too.

225g/8oz medium or fine **oatmeal**
¼ teaspoon **baking soda**
6 tablespoons **water** – hot

Pinch of **salt**
1 dessertspoon of melted **butter**

Preheat the oven to **160C/325F/Gas 3**

Grease and line a baking tray.

Put all your dry ingredients in a bowl and make a well in the centre, now pour in the melted butter and start stirring in the hot water to form a stiff paste.

Knead this dough and roll out thinly (about 2mm) on a floured surface. You can either make a big circle using a plate as your guide and cut this into triangles, or cut out standard rounds with a cookie cutter. Place them on a prepared tray and bake for **approximately 25-30 minutes** or until golden. Let them cool on a wire rack.

You can also cook your oatcakes on an old fashioned girdle or in a heavy based frying pan if you like. Sprinkle the surface with flour and cook on a medium heat for about **3 minutes**. They are ready when the edges start to curl up a little. Now rub the tops with a little more oatmeal and pop them under a hot grill to crisp them up and brown the tops.

rolled oatcakes

This is a modern and slightly posher version of the humble oatcake. The addition of flour gives a milder flavour and they are wonderful with a good strong Orkney cheddar. They are also very quick and easy to make.

210g/7oz **wholemeal flour**
115g/4oz medium **oatmeal**
½ teaspoon **salt**
½ teaspoon **bicarbonate of soda**
90g/3oz **butter**
5-6 tablespoons **water**

coating
1 **egg** beaten
2 tablespoons **oatmeal**

Preheat the oven to **150C/300F/Gas 2**

Grease and line a baking tray.

Whizz up the flour, oatmeal, bicarbonate of soda and salt in your food processor with the butter until you get a breadcrumb type mixture. Now add a little water at a time until you get a dough that you can work with.

Flour your work surface and roll the dough into a sausage shape and wrap in cling film. If you twist either end of the cling film you get a really firm shape. Chill for at least 30 minutes to firm up.

Scatter the oats on a large plate and then whisk up the egg. Using a pastry brush paint the log with the egg and then roll it in the oats. All this handling will have warmed the dough up again and it will be too soft to cut, so rewrap it and pop it back in the fridge to firm up again for another 30 minutes.

Unwrap and using a sharp knife cut off slices of the dough about 4mm thick and bake for **approximately 20 minutes** or until golden.

Makes 25 depending on size.

oatie crunch

An all-time classic and a great stand-by in the biscuit tin. These are loved by young and old alike and are ideal to make when you have a crowd to cater for.

175g/6oz **butter**
275g/9 ¾ oz **demerara sugar**
1 **egg**
4 tablespoons **water**
1 teaspoon **vanilla extract**

375g/13oz **rolled oats**
140g/5oz **plain flour**
1 teaspoon **salt**
½ teaspoon **bicarbonate of soda**

Preheat oven to **180C/350F/Gas 4**

Grease and line a baking tray.

Cream the butter and Demerara sugar until golden and smooth, beat in the egg, vanilla extract and water until well combined.

In a separate bowl mix together all the other dry ingredients and then add them a little at a time to the butter mix. Keep stirring this in and then tip out on to a floured surface. Your oatie mixture should now come together into a firm dough.

Pull off little balls about a tablespoon in volume and place them well apart on your baking tray. You should end up with about 30 biscuits depending on the size you go for.

Bake for **approximately 15 minutes** or until golden brown in colour. Cool on a wire rack.

Makes about 30.

oatie digestives

These are rather like digestive biscuits (graham crackers in USA), a little sweeter than a normal oatcake and taste great with any type of cheese as well as being wonderful just on their own with a nice cup of tea.

75g/2 ½ oz **butter**
115g/4oz medium **oatmeal**
115g/4oz **wholemeal flour**
40g/2oz **light muscovado sugar**

½ teaspoon **bicarbonate of soda**
½ teaspoon **salt**
1 teaspoon **lemon juice**
3 tablespoons **milk**

Preheat the oven to **200C/400F/Gas 6**

Grease and line a baking tray.

Whizz together the butter and dry ingredients in a food processor and add the lemon juice. Now gradually add the milk. You want to bring it all together to form a tacky sort of dough.

Flour your work surface and rolling pin and roll out to about 2-3mm thick. Cut into rounds using a cookie cutter and prick all over with a fork.

Place slightly apart on a lined sheet and bake for **approximately 12-15 minutes** or until browned on the edges only.

Makes approx 14

abernethy biscuits

Funnily enough these are not a biscuit that takes its name from a place in Scotland. They are, in fact, named after one Dr John Abernethy who regularly ate very plain biscuits at his local bakery. He suggested that they should add sugar and caraway seeds to enhance these morsels, and they were such a success they took his name from then on.

225g/8oz **plain flour**
½ teaspoon **baking powder**
90g/3oz **unsalted butter**
90g/3oz **caster sugar**

½ teaspoon **caraway seeds**
1 tablespoon **milk**
1 **egg**

Preheat oven to **190C/375F/Gas 5**

Grease and line a baking sheet.

Sift the flour and baking soda into a large bowl and rub in the butter until everything is well mixed and then add the sugar and caraway seeds. Mix the milk and egg together in a cup and slowly add this to the other ingredients to form a dough.

Tip out on to a floured surface and roll out to approximately 2-3mm. Cut out with round cookie cutters (or use a glass instead). Place slightly apart on the prepared baking sheet and pop into the oven for **10-12 minutes** or until golden on top.

Cool on a wire rack.

brechin heckles

These very plain biscuits were once a favourite in the lunch boxes of workers and school children alike.

225g/8oz **self raising flour**
225g/8oz **plain flour**
165g/6oz **butter**

40g/1½oz **soft brown sugar**
Pinch of **salt**
4 tablespoons **water**

Preheat the oven to **200C/400F/Gas 6**

Grease and line a baking sheet.

Sift both of the flours into a large bowl and rub in the butter until you have a breadcrumb-like mixture. Stir in the salt and sugar and then add the water a little at a time to form a dough.

Roll out on a floured surface to about 3mm and using a 6cm (2½ inch) cookie cutter (or upturned glass) cut out your biscuits.

Space well apart on the baking sheet and bake for **approximately 20 minutes** or until just golden.

Cool on a wire rack and dust with a little sugar.

jammy droppers

No Scottish childhood would be complete without Jammy Dodger biscuits in your snack box for school, at least not in my day. Here is a really easy recipe for making your own homemade version that is far superior to anything you can buy in the shops.

This is a chance to use some of the lovely jam and jelly recipes in this book, be flavourful, anything goes!

90g/3oz **self raising flour**
1 teaspoon **ground cinnamon**
3 tablespoons **cornflour**
70g/2oz **sugar**

70g/2oz **butter** softened
1 **egg** beaten
Jam of choice

Preheat the oven to **180C/350F/Gas 4**

Line a large baking tray with baking paper.

Sift together the flour, cornflour and cinnamon.

In a separate bowl cream the butter and sugar until they are light and fluffy.

Gradually add the egg beating well all the time and then add the flour mixture and fold together until it is all combined but don't overdo it.

Now pull off small pieces of the dough about a teaspoonful at a time and roll into balls. Fill your baking tray with the dough balls (keeping them at least 3cm apart as they will spread when baking) and then gently prod a small indent into each with your finger, don't go right through, you just want a little bowl shape in each and then carefully spoon a drop of jam or jelly into each.

Pop into the oven and bake for **approximately 10 minutes** or until golden. Cool on a wire rack if you can possibly resist them.

Makes about 35.

melting moments

My mum used to make these for us all the time when we were children and my horrid brother used to tease me and tell me that they were baked eyeballs so that I would leave more for him. Luckily I wasn't fooled for long and they became firm favourites with me too.

115g/4oz **butter** softened
150g/5oz **self raising flour**
90g/3oz **caster sugar**
½ teaspoon **vanilla extract**

pinch of **salt**
1 **egg** beaten
25g/1oz **rolled** or **pinhead oats**
4 **glace cherries** quartered

Preheat the oven to **180C/350F/Gas 4**

Grease 2 baking trays.

Beat the butter till it is nice and fluffy and then add the caster sugar and vanilla extract. Sift the flour and salt and add this to the mixture along with the beaten egg. Mix thoroughly to form a soft dough.

Break this up into 16 pieces and roll them into balls just a little bit smaller than a golf ball.

Pour the porridge oats into a saucer and roll each of the dough balls in the oats. Now place each on the baking tray spaced well apart. Push a cherry quarter gently into the centre but don't flatten the balls.

Bake for **approximately 15 minutes** until they turn golden and are well risen. Cool on a wire rack.

Makes about 16.

tantallon cakes

These aren't a cake at all really, they are more of a terribly smart shortbread with the most amazingly zingy lemon flavour. They take their interesting name from Tantallon Castle in the Scottish borders.

115g/4oz **plain flour**
115g/4oz **cornflour**
¼ teaspoon **bicarbonate of soda**
115g/4oz **butter**

115g/4oz **caster sugar**
Grated zest of 1 **lemon**
2 **eggs** beaten

Preheat the oven to **180C/350F/Gas 4**

Grease and line a baking tray.

Sift together the flours and bicarbonate of soda and set this aside. In a large bowl beat the butter with the sugar till it is nice and fluffy and add the eggs and flour mix a little at a time, make sure everything is well blended and add the lemon zest. This should form a dough that is very easy to work with.

Roll out to approximately 2-4mm thick and cut into rounds with a cookie cutter.

Place on a paper covered baking tray and pop into the oven for about **25-30 minutes** or until golden on top.

Sprinkle with sugar and cool on a wire rack.

NOTE; roll thinner (bake less) and serve with good quality vanilla ice cream for a delightful dessert.

Finishing Touches

While scones, pancakes, breads and bannocks (plus all the other bakes of course) are very much the stars of this book, they can be made that wee bit more special with some extra finishing touches.

So here are ten great ideas for jams, jellies, dipping sauces, butters and marmalades, to make things even better.

apple butter

This is not like the butter you'd spread on your bread, fruit butters are more like a rich fruit *purée* and wonderful on your scones and pancakes.

475ml/16fl oz **dry cider**
450g/1lb **cooking apples**
450g/1lb **eating apples**
1 **lemon**

675g/1½lb **granulated sugar**
½ teaspoon **ground cinnamon**
½ teaspoon **mixed spice**

Wash all fruit and peel, core and slice all the apples. Zest the lemon and squeeze out all the juice, set these aside.

Pour the cider into your preserving pan and bring to the boil. Keep it boiling until the liquid has reduced by about half. Now add all the fruit you had set aside earlier.

Cover the pan and cook for 10 minutes, then remove the lid and cook for a further 20 minutes or until all the apples are squishy and tender.

Remove from the heat and allow it all to cool slightly before whizzing up in a food processor to create a *purée*. Press this through a sieve to get a beautifully smooth blend.

Measure the amount of puree you have and put into the preserving pan. Add 275g (10oz) sugar for every 600ml (1 pint) of *purée*. Add the cinnamon and mixed spice at this point and stir well.

Gently heat until all the sugar has dissolved and then raise the temperature and boil for about **20 minutes** stirring all the time. You want to have a thick mixture that will hold its shape when you spoon it on to a cold plate.

Spoon the apple butter into prepared jars and seal. Leave it for a week to let the flavours really develop before using.

Makes about 8 small jars.

bramble butter

The perfect addition to oatcakes and cheese.

350g/11½oz apples
1kg/2lb brambles/blackberries
125ml/4 fl oz water
sugar

Peel and core the apples and cut into chunks, put these into a preserving pan or large pot with the brambles and water and stew until all fruit is tender. Press the stewed fruit through a metal sieve. Weigh the resulting liquid and add an equal quantity of sugar. Return to the pan and heat gently until the sugar dissolves, then increase the heat and boil rapidly. Test for setting point and then give it a few minutes more as you want this to have a good firm texture. Spoon carefully into sterilised jars and seal.

Makes about 6 jars.

250g/8oz butter softened
4 tablespoons chopped fresh parsley and rosemary
1 clove garlic finely chopped
1 tablespoon lemon juice
salt and pepper to taste

herb butter

Mash the butter and blend in the herbs, garlic and lemon juice. Season to taste.

Roll in greaseproof paper and twist the ends tightly, label clearly. Leave in the fridge for at least two hours for the flavours to develop.

Can be stored in the freezer for up to three months. Just cut off what you want to use and pop the rest straight back into the freezer for next time. Great for adding flavour to soups, stews and grills too.

potted cheese

A great way to use up scraps of cheese, especially after Christmas or a party.

350g/12oz cheddar cheese crumbled
75g/3oz butter
½ teaspoon English mustard
Pinch of cayenne pepper
1 tablespoon whisky

It is easiest to use a food processor for this. Just whizz up the cheese and butter until almost smooth. Add mustard, pepper and whisky and whizz again.

Pack tightly into small bowls or wide necked jars. If you are not using it right away cover the top with clarified butter (the top liquid from heated butter) and cover with waxed paper or jar lid.

It will keep for two weeks in the fridge.

raspberry and mint jelly

Scottish raspberries are famed for their flavour and juiciness, I always look forward to raspberry season, whether I'm picking my own crop in the garden or grabbing these gorgeous little gems from the hedgerow, to me they sing of summer and are well worth preserving for the rest of the year too. The addition of mint to this recipe really brings out the full flavour of the fruit and adds to that summer time feeling.

450g/1lb **raspberries**
2 tablespoons chopped fresh **mint** leaves

1 tablespoon **lemon juice**
white sugar

Rinse the raspberries and put them in your preserving pan along with lemon juice. Just cover with water and bring this to the boil and then simmer until the fruit is soft and pulpy.

Pour the fruit into a jelly bag and let it drip overnight.

Measure the resulting juice and for every 600ml (1pint) of juice use 450g (1lb) sugar. Put fruit and sugar into your preserving pan and heat gently until all the sugar has dissolved. Bring to the boil and let it bubble for about 10 minutes or until the setting point (see notes) has been reached.

Let it cool for about 10 minutes and then stir in the chopped mint (this is so that the mint will remain suspended within the jelly and not all float to the top of the jars), pour into sterilised jars and seal.

Makes 2 jars.

rowan berry jelly

Rowan trees are prolific in Scotland, they grow wild in the forests but are now increasingly popular in towns too, even councils plant them along road sides in some areas.

Rowan jelly is excellent served with game and meat, but I like it with oatcakes and cheese, the bitterness really enhances the flavour of goats cheese in particular.

1.8kg/4lb **rowan berries**
1.35kg/3lb **cooking apples**

450g/1lb **granulated sugar** for each 600ml (1 pint) of juice

---

Wash all the fruit and remove the stalks on the berries. Just roughly chop the apples, you don't even need to peel or core them for this easy recipe.

Put all the fruit into a preserving pan and just cover with water. Bring it to the boil and simmer for about 20 minutes, or until all the fruit is soft.

Pour the fruity mixture into a jelly bag (you can easily make your own from muslin or even tights, see notes) and hang over a large bowl to drip all night.

In the morning take down the bag and resist all temptation to squeeze it as this will make your jelly cloudy. Just discard the contents and wash it out for later use. Measure the juice and pour into the preserving pan with the correct amount of sugar (see measurements above), simmer gently for about 10 minutes or until the sugar has completely dissolved. Raise the heat and bring the jelly to a full rolling boil for 5 minutes and then test for setting (see notes). When the jelly has reached setting point spoon it into prepared jars and seal.

Makes approximately 2kg of jelly.

strawberry and redcurrant jam

This brilliantly red confection is summer in a jar. Make lots and keep it to warm up chilly winter days with a blast of sunshine taste. Perfect for scones, pancakes and spreading on biscuits.

750g/1lb 10oz **strawberries**
750g/1lb 10oz **redcurrants**
1.5kg/3lb 5oz **sugar** (caster or granulated)

Juice of 1 **lemon**

Wash all fruit and hull the strawberries (remove the leaves and stalk) and chop in half or quarters if they are very big. Pick off all the stalks from the redcurrants.

Toss all the ingredients into a jam pot (jeely pan in Scotland) or just a large saucepan will do and warm on a low heat to start with as you want all the sugar to dissolve.

Raise the temperature till the fruit mixture starts to boil and bubble but don't stir it (you can wipe down the sides of the pan with a wet pastry brush to push the jam back down into the pot) keep it boiling for about 20 minutes or until it reaches setting point (see notes).

Remove from the heat and give it a gentle stir to make sure no berries are stuck to the bottom of the pan. Leave it for about five minutes to cool slightly before pouring into jars. This helps to keep the berries in suspension so you don't get them all at the top of the jar and nowhere else!

Make sure you have your jars all sterilised and ready and spoon the jam into the jars and seal the lids.

This makes approximately 1.25 litres of jam which will do about 8 small jars.

spiced plum conserve

1kg/2¼lb red plums
1kg/2¼lb granulated sugar
1 tablespoon cinnamon

Wash and stone the plums and half or quarter depending on size and put everything into a large pot or preserving pan.

Add 250ml/8fl oz water and cook over a medium heat until the sugar has all dissolved. Boil rapidly for approximately 5 minutes or until the setting point has been reached.

Carefully spoon into sterilised jars and seal.

Makes 8 small jars.

200g/7oz dark chocolate
(70% cocoa solids)

90g/3oz milk chocolate

2 tablespoons golden syrup

250ml/8fl oz double cream

1 tablespoon whisky

whisky and chocolate dip

Warm everything (apart from the whisky) in microwave or in a small pot on the stove, until it is all melted and mixed together, stir in the whisky.

Serve with Crulla or pancakes.

whisky and ginger marmalade

Scotland in a jar, what more can I say! Scotland is world famous for its marmalade, especially Dundee, where a Mrs Keiller first created it after her husband bought a job lot of cheap Seville oranges from a Spanish ship that had taken refuge in Dundee harbour due to a storm. The oranges were way too bitter to eat so Mrs Keiller made orange jam – the rest is history…

450g/1lb **Seville oranges**
450g/1lb **sweet oranges**
4 **lemons**
3cm/1inch fresh **ginger root**

1.2kg/2½lb **granulated sugar**
1L/2pts **water**
300ml/ ½pt **whisky**

Wash all the fruit and cut in half. Squeeze out all the juice into your preserving pan. Scoop out the flesh and seeds and tie these up in a piece of muslin or other thin cloth and toss into the pan (it all adds to the flavour). Shred up all the skins and add these to the pan as well. Peel and grate the ginger root into the pan. Pour in the water and bring to a boil, cover and simmer for about 2 hours or until the fruit peel is tender. Fish out the muslin bag and squeeze to get all goodness out of it (squash between two saucers as it will be very hot).

Add the sugar and cook over a low heat until the sugar has completely dissolved. Bring it back up to the boil for about 20 minutes or until the setting point has been reached (see notes). Let it cool for about 10 minutes so that the peel will be evenly distributed in the jars. Divide the whisky between the jars and spoon in the marmalade, give each jar a stir to combine and then seal.

Makes about 8 jars.

Notes

index

A
	Abernethy Biscuits	116, 117
	Almond Flory	76, 77
	Apple Butter	127, 128
	Auld Alliance Appley Tart	78, 79

B
	Black Bun	46-48
	Border Tart	80, 81
	Bramble & Apple Frushie	82, 83
	Bramble Berry Bake	49, 50
	Bramble Butter	129
	Breads & Bannocks	19-28
	Brechin Heckles	118, 119
	Broonie	86, 87
	Butterie Rowies	20, 21

C Cranachan Cheesecake 51-53
D Drop Scones 34, 35
Dundee Cake 54, 55
E Easy Bread 28
Edinburgh Gingerbread 88, 89
F Fife Bannock 22, 23
G Gingerbread Husbands 90, 91
Gingernuts 92, 93
Ginger Jacks 84, 85
Glamis Cake 56, 57
H Herb Butter 130
Honey Buns 66, 67
J Jammy Droppers 120, 121
M Marmalade Cake 58, 59
Melting Moments 122, 123
Montrose Cakes 68, 69
Morning Rolls 24, 25
O Oatcakes Basic 108, 109
Oatcakes Rolled 110, 111
Oatie Crunch 112, 113
Oatie Digestives 114, 115

P Parlies 94, 95
Petticoat Tails 100, 101
Porridge Pancakes 70, 71
Potted Cheese 131
R Raspberry & Mint Jelly 132, 133
Rowan Berry Jelly 134, 135
S Sair Heidies 72, 73
Scones 29-44
Scones Cheesy Herb 32, 33
Scones Drop 34, 35
Scones Fruit 36, 37
Scones Simple 30, 31
Scones Soda 38, 39
Scones Tattie 40, 41
Scones Tea 44
Scones Treacle 42, 43
Scotch Pancakes 34, 35
Scottish Snowballs 74, 75
Scottish Tea Loaf 60, 61
Seed Cake 62, 63
Selkirk Bannock 26, 27
Shortbread 96-107
Ayrshire Shortbread 96, 97
Millionaires Shortbread 98, 99
Petticoat Tails 100, 101
Shortbread Sandwich 102, 103
Simple Shortbread 104, 105
Strawberry Shorties 106, 107
Spiced Plum Conserve 138
Strawberry & Redcurrant Jam 136, 137
T Tantallon Cakes 124, 125
W Whisky & Chocolate
Dipping Sauce 139
Whisky Marmalade 140, 141